The Night The World Turned ROYAL BLUE

THE ROAD TO THE WORLD SERIES

KANSAS CITY VS. OAKLAND
SEPTEMBER 30, 2014
KAUFFMAN STADIUM, KC

WILD CARD GAME

SEC 225 EE
ROW 04
SEAT

Written by **Jason Sivewright**
Illustrations by **Kristen & Kevin Howdeshell**

In a land full of pinstripes and mean birds of red
Monsters of green and tigers to dread,
Stood one band of misfits, long since forgotten
Who, year upon year, had

Simply
been
rotten.

The joy that once rose, from the founts of "The K"
Had, for 29 years, slowly faded away.
The legends of Howser, King George, and Bo
Were now distant whispers, from long long ago.

All of this changed, one cool Autumn night
When the lights of the land, for a moment shone bright.
On Hosmer & Cain and all of our crew
'Twas the night that the world
turned deep, royal blue.

Beane's boys from the west had bagged up their ace
In hopes of securing their postseason place
By dusting our boys in blue to the side
But
"Big Game" James
33
had a battle in mind.

Back and forth, forth and back, the tussle did sway.

Beane's boys hit like hammers, as we chipped away.

"Big Game" was pulled from the fray too soon,

And the very next blow was a deafening BOOM!

The fountains fell silent,
 no fan uttered a word

The fate of our band
of misfits assured.

Yet no one bothered to mention
to them

That there was no way
they could come back

and win!

Two singles each, trailed with two swipes of a base
Led to Beane's boys quickly pulling their ace.
As Hosmer slid home, the whole land sat stunned
For those boys from the west
only led by one run!

'Twas the end of the ninth and "the K" sat entranced
Sir Willingham singled to give us a chance.
Aoki came up to the plate, sword unsheathed
But our true hope lived in the
feet of a thief.

Dyson mounted his steed,

and to second he flew

Before Beane's boys knew it, he'd taken third too!

With Aoki's sac fly, the good guys in blue

Tied it all up,

cause

that's what speed do!

The Battle went on,
all was even again

Then Ned waved a hand to bring in Young Finn.

He would face Mighty Moss, the mountain of clout,

Too bad for O-town,
Young Finn struck him out!

Two frames were lost, with ninety feet left to go,
But they just couldn't land the triumphant blow.
In the top of the twelfth Old Alberto stepped in
With a line shot to left
            he assured the A's' win.

A soft grounder from Cain left us two outs away

From all that blue hope quickly fading to grey

Then up came **Prince Hosmer** who just wouldn't quit

A shot off the wall, kept the dying fire lit.

WHOMP!

Then into the box stepped Christian Colón.
He bounced a ball skyward and
                    singled Hos home.

Colón then took second,
        after Gordo flew out

With the battle tied up,
    we were down to one out.

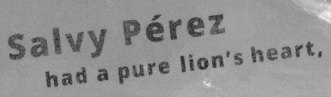

Salvy Pérez
had a pure lion's heart,

But most of his swings seemed
doomed
from the start.

A wave at a slider, a fastball blown by
Left the fans at "The K" always
wondering
"why?"

So of course it would be, there was no other way,

It fell to **Big Salvy** to save us the day.

'Twas a ball too outside, for a batter to touch

Salvy lined it to left, past a diving A's glove.

Colón trotted home, and the roar grew **and** grew.

It was that very moment the world turned royal blue.

King George rose with joy, as his seat he passed down,

And on went our boys to reclaim the crown!

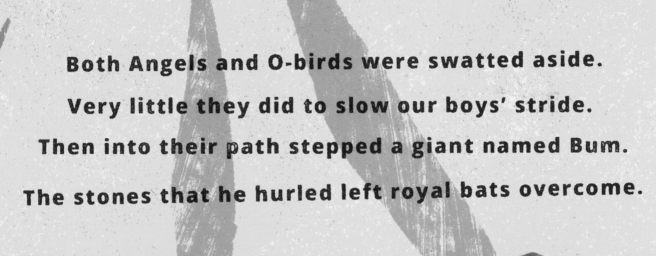

Both Angels and O-birds were swatted aside.

Very little they did to slow our boys' stride.

Then into their path stepped a giant named Bum.

The stones that he hurled left royal bats overcome.

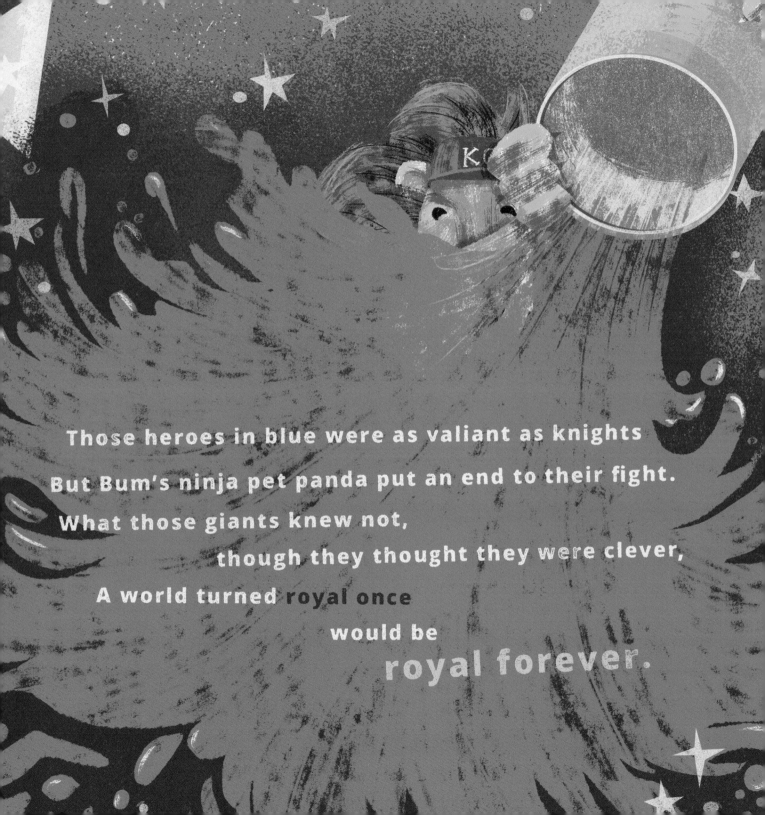

Those heroes in blue were as valiant as knights
But Bum's ninja pet panda put an end to their fight.
What those giants knew not,
  though they thought they were clever,
A world turned royal once
  would be
  royal forever.

2014

The retelling of a game that will go down in franchise history.
Dedicated to all Kansas City fans, but especially the little ones,
Isaiah Sivewright and Emerson and Vera Howdeshell.

CPSIA information can be obtained
at www.ICGtesting.com
Printed in the USA
LVIC04n2348210815
451140LV00022B/146